IMAGES OF
MOVIE STARS

IMAGES OF
MOVIE STARS

Tim Hill

Photographs by the
Daily Mail

This is a Parragon Publishing Book
First published in 2005

Parragon Publishing
Queen Street House
4 Queen Street
Bath, BA1 IHE, UK

Photographs © Associated Newspapers Ltd
and GettyImages (see page 224 for details)
Text © Parragon 2005

Produced by Atlantic Publishing

ISBN 1-40545-321-4
Printed in China

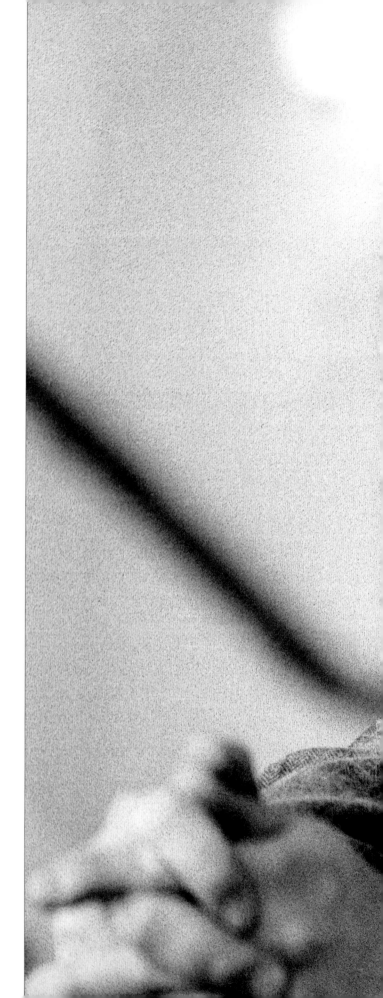

INTRODUCTION

In the early Hollywood days actors were anonymous and uncredited, working for a pittance. Mary Pickford—"America's Sweetheart"—began her career on $10 a day. But the studios soon discovered that actors could sell movies. They began poaching their rivals' talent, then hyped up their expensive acquisitions. Pickford, a bigger draw even than Chaplin, eventually made $350,000 per movie. The star system was born.

Images of Movie Stars features a host of silver screen legends of the past century, the likes of Garbo, Cagney, Gable, and Hepburn—from an era when MGM boasted "more stars than the firmament"—to their modern counterparts: Cruise, de Niro, Streep, Schwarzenegger. This collection of stunning photographs from the archives of the *Daily Mail,* along with the detailed commentary, provide a wealth of information on the stars' public and private faces. It is an indispensable addition to the movie fans' collection.

IMAGES OF
MOVIE STARS

EPIC BUDGETS

Opposite: Charlton Heston at the premiere of *Ben Hur*. The budget was an epic $15 million, a new high watermark in movie history. The investment paid off; it won six Oscars, including the Best Picture of 1959. Heston also won an Oscar, though he only got the part after MGM failed to attract Burt Lancaster, Rock Hudson and Brando.

Left: The nephew of actress-singer Rosemary Clooney, George Clooney turned to acting after failing to make it as a major league baseball player. He shot to fame in the TV medical drama *ER* and went on to corner the market in suave, loveable rogues. *Ocean's Eleven*, a typical Clooney role, earned him $20 million.

BACALL DEVELOPS "THE LOOK"

Opposite: Lauren Bacall was an unknown 19-year-old when she tested for *To Have And Have Not*, the famous "whistle" scene. She was so nervous about playing opposite Bogart, 25 years her senior and a big star, that she developed the mannerism of holding her chin down and glancing up. Dubbed "The Look", it was in fact a defensive technique, purely to stop herself from shaking.

Above: Tony Curtis was a studio-manufactured star whose early pictures traded on his pretty-boy looks. He went on to give some fine performances, notably in *Some Like It Hot,* in which his pursuit of Marilyn Monroe included a marvelous parody of Cary Grant.

SEX KITTEN TO OSCAR WINNER

Jane Fonda's early career was something of a hit-and-miss affair. She was the feisty schoolteacher who employed drunken gunslinger Lee Marvin in *Cat Ballou*; and newly married to Robert Redford in Neil Simon's *Barefoot In the Park*, which brought forth comparisons to the Powell/Loy repartee a generation earlier. But in *Barbarella* —directed by her then-husband Roger Vadim—it was her sex appeal which was to the fore. Fonda gave a stunning performance in *They Shoot Horses Don't They?*, a movie about the dance marathons of the Depression era. She missed out on an Oscar that time, but was named Best Actress for her next picture, *Klute*, in which she played a hooker to Donald Sutherland's cop. There was a second Oscar for her performance as an army wife who falls for a wounded Vietnam vet in *Coming Home*. One role she missed out on was Karen Silkwood. Fonda unsuccessfully tried to acquire the rights to the story about the nuclear industry whistle-blower who died in mysterious circumstances. *Silkwood* was eventually filmed with Meryl Streep in the title role.

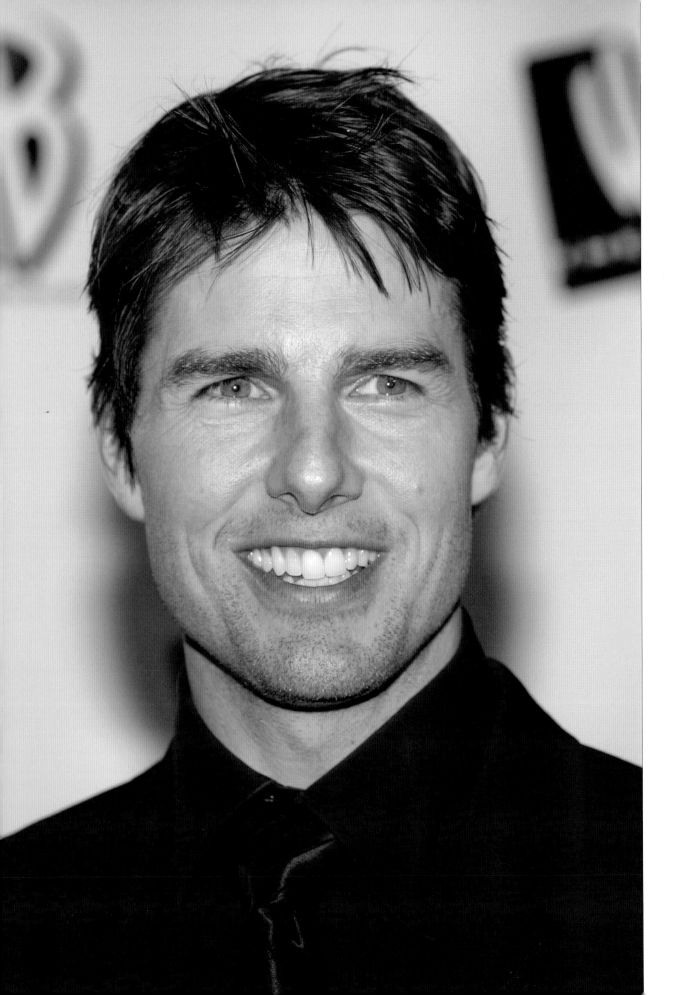

FROM PRIEST TO HEART-THROB

Left: Born in 1962 in Syracuse, New York, Cruise was already a top box-office star, in the 80s having made some of the biggest-grossing movies of that decade including *Top Gun* and *Rain Man*.

By the 1990s he was one of the highest paid actors in the world earning more than $10 million a picture in such blockbuster hits as *Interview with the Vampire*, *Mission: Impossible* and *Jerry Maguire*. He was married to actress Nicole Kidman until 2001. The Hollywood heart-throb was a far cry from his first calling: Cruise entered a seminary, intending to train for the priesthood.

Opposite: Uma Thurman attends the Marc Jacobs Fall 2005 show during Olympus Fashion Week at The Armory in New York City. Thurman, whose mother was a Swedish model, was discovered at the age of 16 by photographer Norman Parkinson. She received more than $20 million for her two *Kill Bill* movies.

DAVIS BUCKS GLAMOR TREND

Left: From an early age Bette Davis set her sights on becoming a great actress. She bucked the trend of 1930s Hollywood, which saw beauty and glamor as an actress's primary assets. Davis wanted meaty, disparate roles worthy of her talents. Her breakthrough came in the 1934 movie *Of Human Bondage*. RKO wanted to borrow her from Warner Bros. to play the scheming waitress Mildred, and she relentlessly pestered Jack Warner to gain his permission. Davis was outstanding,

although it was for her performance in *Dangerous* the following year that she won her first Oscar. She was nominated on nine other occasions, winning the award for *Jezebel*. Only Katherine Hepburn was honored more by her peers.

Above: Bette Davis strolling down a country Lane in Hurley in Berkshire, England where she stayed in June 1958.

ARNIE OUTDOES BOYHOOD HERO

Arnold Schwarzenegger followed in the footsteps of his boyhood hero Steve Reeves, who also turned to acting after winning the Mr. Universe title. Both were given roles which made full use of their physical prowess; but while Reeves' career petered out after cutting a dash in roles such as Hercules, Schwarzenegger rose to become the No. 1 box office draw. He was fortunate in coming to prominence in the era of the big blockbuster—and none came bigger than the *Terminator* films. By the early 1990s he had supplanted Sylvester Stallone and Eddie Murphy as Hollywood's top male star, his movies having grossed over $1 billion. There were amiable diversions into comedy along the way, in vehicles such as *Twins* and *Kindergarten Cop*, but Arnie built his reputation—and sizeable bank balance— primarily on high-octane comic-strip adventures. After a decade at the top the body count he was personally responsible for was already approaching 300 and rising.

NOVICE HOWARD FOR BRIEF ENCOUNTER LEAD

Above: Trevor Howard, a fine actor and celebrated party animal. He had had minor roles in just two movies when Noel Coward chose him for the male lead in *Brief Encounter*. Co-star Celia Johnson was nominated for an Oscar, as was director David Lean. It set the pattern for Howard's career, which was full of memorable if not award-winning

performances, though he did receive an Oscar nomination for his role in the 1960 adaptation of *Sons And Lovers*.

Opposite: Howard with Mel Brooks, who regarded his 1974 movie *Blazing Saddles* as a ground-breaking big-screen comedy.

DEPP DEBUTS AS ELM STREET VICTIM

Johnny Depp came to acting after a chance meeting with Nicholas Cage, who suggested he might be good in front of a camera. He made his debut as one of Freddy Krueger's victims in *Nightmare On Elm Stree*t, but it was the 1990 movie *Edward Scissorhands* that established his reputation. It was the first of several collaborations with Tim Burton; *Ed Wood* and *Sleepy Hollow* followed in the 1990s. Music was Depp's first passion. He is said to have based Captain Jack Sparrow—the character he played in *Pirates of the Caribbean: The Curse Of The Black Pearl*—on rock legend Keith Richards. He also once filled in on guitar with Oasis for an incapacitated Noel Gallagher.

Right: Depp and wife Vanessa Paradis arrive at the 11th Annual Screen Actors Guild Awards on February 5 2005 in Los Angeles. On May 27 1999 Depp became a father for the first time when Vanessa gave birth to their daughter, Lily-Rose Melody Depp. A son, Jack, was born in 2002.

Opposite: Depp with former girlfriend Kate Moss.

FROM OBSCURITY TO SUPERHERO

Christopher Reeve (pictured right with wife Dana) had had just one minor role —in the submarine drama *Gray Lady Down*—when he was chosen to play the most famous comic strip hero of them all. He reprised the Superman role three times over the next decade, and was naturally concerned about typecasting. Reeve consulted Sean Connery on the subject, the quintessential James Bond replying: "First you have to be good enough that they ask you to play it again and again." Reeve took his craft very seriously. He'd attended New York's famous Juilliard School of Performing Arts, where he roomed with Robin Williams. Between Superman movies he sought out intelligent roles. An adaptation of Henry James' *The Bostonians* held more appeal than *The Running Man* and *Total Recall*, both of which went to Schwarzenegger after he turned them down. In *Above Suspicion*, one of his final pictures prior to his riding accident in 1995, Reeve played a paralyzed man. He died on October 10 2004.

THANKS FOR THE MEMORY...

Opposite: Bob Hope is mobbed by autograph hunters on a trip to London in 1939. Hope was already a radio star when he turned his hand to movies. His debut, in *The Big Broadcast Of 1938* , provided him with his famous signature tune, "Thanks For The Memory", which won an Academy Award. The comedy thriller *The Cat and the Canary* (1939) established his screen persona: brash but with a yellow streak a mile wide. The most famous vehicles for that screen character were the "Road" movies, a series which began with *The Road To Singapore* in 1940. Hope did the wisecracks, Bing Crosby did the songs and invariably got Dorothy Lamour.

Above: Hope and Crosby indulging their passion for golf in 1952.

SLOW RISE TO THE TOP

Although he was a keen amateur actor, Kevin Costner looked set for a business career when a chance meeting with Richard Burton set him on course for Hollywood. It took him years to get a foothold on the ladder; one of his many jobs was doing bus tours of the stars' homes. When he finally got a break, in the satirical comedy *The Big Chill* (1983), his scenes ended up on the cutting-room floor. The movie's writer-director Lawrence Kasdan remembered Costner, however, and cast him in his 1985 movie about 19th century pioneers, *Silverado*. By 1990 Costner was an A-list star, but even so Hollywood refused him the money to make a three-hour western. A British company stepped in to back *Dances With Wolves*, which won Costner the Best Director Oscar and a nomination for Best Actor. It also picked up the Best Picture award.

BOGARDE MURDERS DIXON

In one of his early movies, *The Blue Lamp*, Dirk Bogarde played the petty crook who shot George Dixon, the amiable policeman who was later resurrected for a long-running TV series. It was his portrayal of Dr. Simon Sparrow, a series which began with *Doctor in the House* in 1954, that made Bogarde Britain's top box office star. He became disillusioned with the insubstantial roles Rank was offering him. *Victim* (1961) was a notable exception, Bogarde playing a lawyer in the first movie to deal overtly with homosexuality. *I Could Go On Singing* was essentially a vehicle for Judy Garland (right) to perform on stage, but Bogarde stole the show as her boorish husband. He arguably gave his finest performance in the 1971 film of Thomas Mann's novel *Death in Venice*, playing a composer who becomes fixated on a young boy.

Right: Judy Garland was signed to MGM at the age of thirteen, and first came to the public eye when she appeared in *Broadway Melody of 1938*. However, it was her role as Dorothy in *The Wizard of Oz* in 1939 that launched her career as a star, resulting in an honorary Oscar for her outstanding performance as a screen juvenile. Further successes such as *Meet Me in St. Louis*, *Easter Parade* in 1948 and *A Star is Born* in 1954 followed, but Garland was continually dogged by personal struggles. She died in 1969 of an overdose of sleeping pills.

FIRST BEAUTY QUEEN TO WIN OSCAR

Sophia Loren trod a well-worn path from beauty queen and model to actress. However, she was the first to rise to the top of her new profession, winning an Academy Award for her performance in the 1960 movie *Two Women*. It was one of many pictures in which she was directed by Vittorio de Sica, from whom she learned most about the craft of acting. The other great influence on her career was producer Carlo Ponti, whom she met when she was 14. It was he who changed her name from Scicolone to Loren and orchestrated her rise to become one of the screen's great international stars and sex symbols. They married in 1957, the year Ponti got Loren her first Hollywood starring role, opposite Cary Grant and Frank Sinatra in *The Pride and the Passion*.

SINATRA TAKES PAY CUT TO SECURE MAGGIO ROLE

Above: Howard Hawks christened Lauren Bacall as well as directed her in her debut movie, *To Have And Have Not;* he decided Betty wasn't right for the burgeoning star. Frank Sinatra was already a household name as a crooner when he turned to acting. By the early 1950s his career in both fields had nosedived. He was so desperate for the part of Maggio in *From Here to Eternity* that he cut his fee from $150,000 to

$8,000. His performance earned him a Best Supporting Actor Oscar. He was also nominated for an award for the 1955 movie *The Man With The Golden Arm.*

Opposite: David Niven, Ava Gardner and Stewart Granger were shipwrecked members of the eternal triangle in 1957 comedy *The Little Hut.*

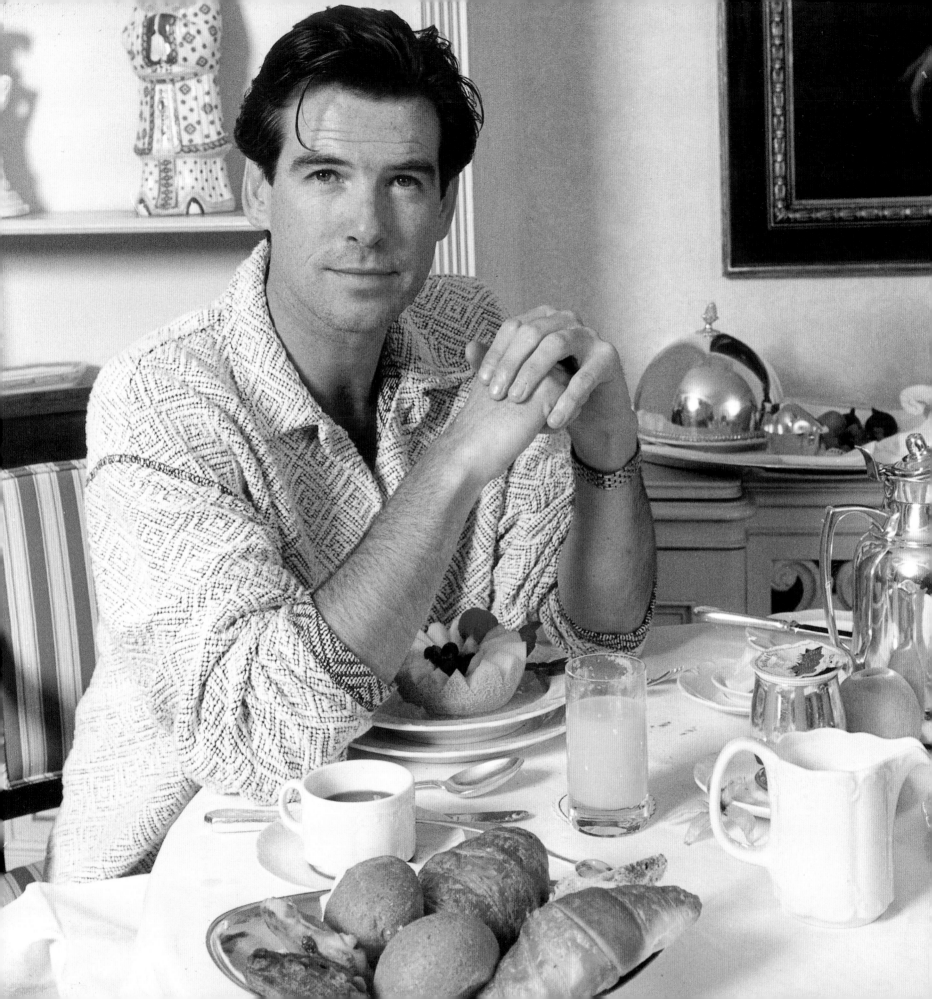

IN THE FOOTSTEPS OF MR. BOND

Irish born Pierce Brosnan has rejuvenated the role of the quintessential Englishman, the British Secret Service Agent, James Bond. Earmarked to take the part of 007 after Roger Moore retired from the role in 1986, he missed out on the opportunity because he was still under contract to make a series of Remington Steele, the show that brought him to public prominence. It was not until 1995 that the man voted "Sexiest Man Alive" in 2001 finally got to play James Bond in *Golden Eye*.

He has since reprised the Bond role in a further three movies: *Tomorrow Never Dies, The World Is Not Enough* and *Die Another Day*. But, although he has become firmly identified as Mr. James Bond, and even purchased the typewriter on which Ian Fleming wrote the Bond novels, he has had experience enough on stage and television, as well as in movies, where he has played an enormous range of parts, to avoid being overshadowed by the character.

SON OF THE SWASHBUCKLING KING

Douglas Fairbanks Jr. (pictured left with his second wife) was the first movie star who had to deal with illustrious forebears. His father had been the swashbuckling king of Hollywood in the silent era, his step-mother was Mary Pickford; between them they had helped found United Artists. Fairbanks Jr. had no great passion for acting, but he had a name the studios could exploit, was extremely handsome and had a marvelous voice—a major asset as talkies took off. He was briefly married to Joan Crawford, whose much greater ambition rubbed off on him. He emerged from his father's shadow with action adventures such as *The Prisoner of Zenda*, *Gunga Din* and *Sinbad the Sailor*, the last of these being the most financially successful movie of his career.

"CALL ME MISTER TIBBS"

Sidney Poitier (pictured opposite with future wife Joanna Shimkus) was the first internationally acclaimed black actor. His debut picture, *No Way Out* (1950), was the first major movie to deal with color prejudice. His youthful looks got him a part as a student in *The Blackboard Jungle*—even though he was then 30. He won an Oscar for the 1963 movie *Lilies of the Field* but 1967 was his golden year. He played the educated New York detective Virgil Tibbs to Rod Steiger's hard-bitten Southern police chief in *In The Heat of the Night*; and the man Katharine Houghton brings home to meet parents Spencer Tracy and Katharine Hepburn in *Guess Who's Coming to Dinner?* His performances made him the top US draw in 1968.

THE DIMINUTIVE TOUGH GUY

Alan Ladd's diminutive frame—he stood just 5ft 6in—didn't stop him from becoming one of the screen's great tough guys. He served a long apprenticeship, on radio and in bit-part movie roles, together with a host of menial jobs when even these weren't forthcoming. *This Gun For Hire*, made in 1942, elevated him to star status. This was the first of several pictures in which Ladd was teamed with Veronica Lake, their chemistry proving very popular at the box office. He is pictured (left) in the 1953 war movie *The Red Beret;* that same year he made the classic western with which he is most enduringly associated, *Shane.* Ladd excelled as the gunfighter trying to change his ways but forced to fight fire with fire to help a peaceful town under threat.

RELUCTANT SAGE NETS A FORTUNE

Alec Guinness is one of the great character actors of stage and screen. His early career was under the tutelage of John Gielgud, who gave him both inspiration and confidence. In the 1940s he made two Dickens classics under director David Lean. His casting as Herbert Pocket in *Great Expectations* was unsurprising, Guinness reprising a role he had played on stage; but he had to fight to convince Lean that he could pull off the role of Fagin in the 1948 adaptation of *Oliver Twist*. It was a tour de force. In the 1950s he appeared in a string of Ealing comedy classics: *The Lavender Hill Mob*, *The Man in the White Suit* and *The Ladykillers*. It was another collaboaration with Lean which brought him his first Oscar. The role of Colonel Nicholson in *The Bridge on the River Kwai* was first offered to Noel Coward. Guinness gave a remarkable performance as the man in charge of British POWs in a Japanese prison camp. He was knighted two years later, in 1959. Guinness was initially loath to play the sage knight in *Star Wars*. George Lucas thanked him with 2.5 percent of the the take, which made him a fortune as the movie broke all box office records.

AND VADIM CREATED BARDOT

Roger Vadim's 1956 film *And God Created Woman* made his then-wife Brigitte Bardot an international sex symbol, and created a storm of protest from many who felt it was an affront to decency and a further step on the way to moral decline. Some movie theater managers in America risked jail in showing a picture about an oversexed teenager taking every opportunity to bare her flesh against an exotic St. Tropez backdrop. La Bardot herself would come to abhor her sex kitten image.

COPPOLA FIGHTS PACINO'S CAUSE

Francis Ford Coppola had to fight hard to get Al Pacino the role of Michael Corleone in *The Godfather*—and even harder to prevent him from being replaced during shooting. The studio bosses wanted a bigger name; Pacino had made just two movies, neither of which had made him a household name. The two *Godfather* films did. Pacino's critically acclaimed performances made him one of Hollywood's hottest properties. In between he had made *Serpico*, the true story of a New York cop out to expose corruption. He was on the other side of the law in *Dog Day Afternoon* (1975), playing an incompetent bank robber in another Sidney Lumet picture inspired by real events. It meant that Pacino had been nominated for an Oscar four years running. The long overdue Best Actor award finally came in 1992, for *Scent of a Woman*.

PECK TURNS DOWN *HIGH NOON*

Left: Gregory Peck emerged as one of Hollywood's great leading men in the 1940s. David O. Selznick was unimpressed by an early screen test, but would go on to produce a number of Peck's most famous movies, including *Spellbound*, *The Paradine Case* and *Duel in the Sun*. Peck famously turned down *High Noon*, feeling that it mirrored too closely his 1950 picture *The Gunfighter*. Gary Cooper's portrayal of Will Kane won him an Oscar. A decade later Peck picked up the Best Actor award for his performance as Atticus Finch in *To Kill a Mockingbird*.

Opposite: Dorothy Parker once dismissed one of Katherine Hepburn's stage performances with the withering line: "She ran the gamut of emotions from A to B." But in the 1930s Hepburn came closest to challenging Garbo as Hollywood's queen. She won an Oscar for *Morning Glory*, only her third movie; almost half a century later she picked up her fourth, playing opposite Henry Fonda in *On Golden Pond*.

DE NIRO INHERITS BRANDO MANTLE

It was perhaps fitting that Robert de Niro won his first Academy Award for his portrayal of the young Vito Corleone in *The Godfather Part II*. Marlon Brando had played the ageing patriarch in the first movie—the only time that two actors have won an Oscar playing the same role. Many would come to regard de Niro as Brando's successor in a wider sphere: not only as the greatest actor of his generation but as the actor who held a mirror up to American society. He gave an electrifying performance as Travis Bickle in *Taxi Driver,* and won the Best Actor award for another Martin Scorsese picture, *Raging Bull*, the story of boxing legend Jake La Motta. De Niro is famous for immersing himself in a role. He spent months perfecting the Sicilian accent for his role in *The Godfather*, while to play the out-of-shape La Motta he put on 50lb.

HAMMER'S BROODING STAR

With his dark, brooding appearance and faint air of menace, Oliver Reed was well suited to the Hammer horror roles he played in the early part of his career. A nephew of director Carol Reed, he was a suitably nasty Bill Sikes in *Oliver!*, the surprise Best Picture of 1968. He appeared in two Ken Russell movies, *Women In Love* and *The Devils,* but his attempts to crack Hollywood revealed that his acting ability fell short of his undeniable screen presence. He became a notorious bon viveur, often boorish on the chat show circuit, though he continued to be in demand as an actor. He died in 1999, while playing Proximo in Ridley Scott's *Gladiator.*

THE WORLD'S MOST BEAUTIFUL WOMAN

Ava Gardner and Frank Sinatra were married in 1951. It was second time round for Sinatra, while Gardner had already had two celebrity marriages, to Mickey Rooney and bandleader Artie Shaw. Her third was a tempestuous affair, which ended long before she and Sinatra divorced in 1957. Gardner had arrived in Hollywood in 1941. She had no acting experience but an MGM screen test showed that the camera loved her. Hailed as "the world's most beautiful woman", she was under no illusions about her acting ability. But the fans made her a star and her exotic allure endured long after her physical charms had faded.

OSCAR-WINNING PERFORMANCE

Opposite: Jodie Foster was one of the few child stars who enjoyed continued success in adulthood. She gave an Oscar-winning performance as a rape victim in the 1988 movie *The Accused*, and three years later won a second award for her role as federal agent Clarice Starling in *Silence Of The Lambs*.

Left: As the daughter of Jon Voight, Angelina Jolie knew more than most about Hollywood. Before achieving huge success for her best known role in *Lara Croft: Tomb Raider* and a catalog of 30 other movies, Jolie appeared in music videos and worked as a model in London.

HOOKER ROLE SETS JODIE ON ROAD TO STARDOM

Thirteen-year-old Jodie Foster, pictured in 1976. Foster appeared in TV commercials at the age of two and made her movie debut at eight. She had a string of credits to her name by the time she played hooker Iris in *Taxi Driver*, for which she was nominated as Best Supporting Actress. 1976 also saw her star as Tallulah in *Bugsy Malone*, an early indication of the range of an actress who had no formal acting training. She was first choice to play Princess Leia in *Star Wars* but her Disney contract prevented her from taking the part.

MCQUEEN V NEWMAN

Opposite: Chess was never the same after the game Steve McQueen and Faye Dunaway played in the heist caper *The Thomas Crown Affair*. McQueen vied with Paul Newman as the top box-office draw during the late '60s and early '70s. When the two teamed up for the 1974 disaster movie *The Towering Inferno,* the competitive edge was extraordinary: both received $1 million plus 20 percent of the gross receipts; both had exactly the same number of lines; and both were able to claim top billing. The latter problem was resolved by having the name on the right-hand side of the posters set above that on the left: thus each star's name appeared first, depending on whether you read right-to-left or top-to-bottom.

Right: Tom Cruise and Nicole Kidman, Hollywood's golden couple in the 1990s.

STARTLING BRITISH SUCCESS

Opposite: Hugh Grant toasting the success of his meteoric rise to stardom at the premiere of the worldwide box-office smash *Four Weddings and a Funeral.* With him is actress and girlfriend of 13 years (1987-2000), Liz Hurley. "We are completely startled by its success" admitted scriptwriter Richard Curtis. The very British movie that took America by storm, and also made it to No.1 in France and Australia, was just the platform Grant's career required. Five years later Hugh Grant repeated the success of *Four Weddings* in *Notting Hill* in the role of bookshop owner William Thacker, alongside Julia Roberts. The main difference for Grant was that he earned $100,000 for *Four Weddings* but more than $7 million for *Notting Hill.*

"JUST KNOW YOUR LINES AND DON'T BUMP INTO THE FURNITURE"

Spencer Tracy didn't possess the physical attributes to rival the likes of Gable or Grant, but many of his peers regarded him as the greatest screen actor of his generation, some maintain of all time. He was more self-effacing on the subject: "Just know your lines and don't bump into the furniture." Even in vehicles that weren't top notch Tracy was never anything other than first-rate. He won Oscars in successive years for *Captains Courageous* and *Boys' Town*. The 1942 movie *Woman of the Year*, co-starring Katherine Hepburn, launched one of the great on-screen partnerships. On first meeting she said: "I'm afraid I'm too tall for you Mr. Tracy," to which he replied: "Don't worry, Miss Hepburn, I'll soon cut you down to size."

THE GREATEST SCREEN VILLAIN

Anthony Hopkins had a classical training, studying at the Royal Academy of Dramatic Art and working at the National Theatre under Laurence Olivier. His early movie career showed his range: he was the benign doctor trying to prevent John Hurt from being consigned to freak show exhibit in *The Elephant Man*; and he was suitably chilling as the ventriloquist obsessed with his dummy in *Magic*. It was an even more disturbing role, Hannibal Lecter in *Silence of the Lambs*, that brought Hopkins an Academy Award. He was not on screen for very long but his bravura performance as psychopath Lecter was regarded by many as the greatest ever portrayal of screen villainy. He was knighted in 1993, the year in which he was also Oscar nominated for a very different role in *Remains of the Day*.

FANS REFUSE TO ACCEPT GRANT AS KILLER

The words "urbane" and "suave" might have been invented with Cary Grant in mind. Although by common consent his range was limited, he had marvelous comic timing, as shown in movies such as *Bringing Up Baby, His Girl Friday* and *Arsenic And Old Lace*. In the 1941 Hitchcock movie *Suspicion*, Grant killed Joan Fontaine in the original cut, but preview audiences simply refused to accept him in the role of murderer and a more palatable ending was shot. His popularity endured through to the 1960s, and at the end of that decade he was awarded a special lifetime achievement Oscar.

ENGLISH ROSE

Kate Winslett has acting in her blood. Both parents were stage actors as are her two sisters. Her big break came in 1995 when she successfully auditioned for the part of Marianne Dashwood in *Sense and Sensibility* for which she won a British Academy Award and an Oscar nomination for Best Supporting Actress. But the role that made her a household name was as the aristocratic Rose Dewitt Bukater opposite Leonardo DiCaprio in James Cameron's 1997 epic *Titanic*. In 1998 she married James Threapleton, and gave birth to daughter, Mia, in October 2000. Now married to director Sam Mendes and with a second child Joe, Winslett has established herself as one of the world's leading actresses.

THE LONG ROAD TO SUPERSTARDOM

Michael Douglas's early career gave little indication that he would become one of Hollywood's most bankable stars. When he turned to television as sidekick to his father's old friend Karl Malden in *The Streets of San Francisco*, Douglas himself wondered if he would ever return to the big screen. It was as a producer that he first hit the big time, with *One Flew Over The Cuckoo's Nest* and *The China Syndrome*. Despite these huge successes, there followed a lengthy fallow period at Columbia. He was interested in making a movie about an extra-terrestrial, and a swashbuckling adventure. Spielberg beat him to it in both cases, with *ET* and *Raiders of the Lost Ark*. After leaving Columbia, Douglas sold the idea for *Romancing The Stone* to Twentieth Century Fox, the picture which launched him on the road to superstardom.

FAITH PAYS OFF

For a decade Kirk Douglas tried to get Ken Kesey's novel *One Flew Over The Cuckoo's Nest* onto the big screen. He had played Randall McMurphy on Broadway and owned the movie rights but couldn't get the backing to get the project off the ground. It eventually passed from father to son, and although Michael Douglas (opposite) got the money together he had problems in getting stars interested in such a delicate subject matter. Brando and Hackman refused the lead role, while Anne Bancroft and Jane Fonda were among those who turned down the part of the authoritarian Nurse Ratched. Jack Nicholson and Louise Fletcher took the roles and both gave Oscar-winning performances. *One Flew Over The Cuckoo's Nest* won five Oscars in total, including Best Motion Picture, and grossed $200 million.

Above: Michael Douglas with his wife Catherine Zeta-Jones, who won an Oscar for her part in the movie *Chicago*. The couple married in November 2000.

"OUR GRACIE"

Left: It is difficult to overstate how big a star Gracie Fields was in the 1930s. Her record sales were phenomenal, and when she turned to movies—when she was over 30—audiences flocked to see feel-good vehicles for the Lancashire lass. Fields was a fine comedienne, though there was no hint of the sexual frisson generated by a Garbo or a Mae West; the emphasis was on the wholesome, not the provocative. It was a formula which at one point made her the world's highest paid entertainer. Hollywood thought her style wouldn't travel but eventually relented. The breakthrough didn't quite materialize, and Fields—for whom Hollywood held no attraction—went into semi-retirement by emigrating to the island of Capri.

Opposite: Gracie Fields (second from the left) and her three understudies in *The Show's the Thing.*

FROM SHAKESPEARE TO BOND

Considering film is not her preferred medium, Judi Dench has reached extraordinary heights in her career in movies. She received a Best Actress Oscar nomination for her portrayal of Queen Victoria in *Mrs. Brown*, and for the lead role in *Iris*, a movie which depicted novelist Iris Murdoch's struggle with Alzheimer's disease. She finally won the coveted award for her supporting role in *Shakespeare In Love*, despite appearing on screen as Queen Elizabeth for just eight minutes. Dench's range is remarkable, spanning TV comedy, all the great Shakespearean roles and regular appearances in the Bond blockbusters as M.

TINSELTOWN'S PRINCESS

If Hollywood was Tinseltown, Grace Kelly was its fairytale princess. She made just 11 movies in five years, before retiring to become Princess Grace of Monaco. The Kelly canon was short but impressive: in only her second picture she played Gary Cooper's wife in *High Noon*; she was nominated as Best Supporting Actress for *Mogambo,* playing opposite Gable; then came *Rear Window*, the first of three Hitchcock movies. Kelly won an Oscar for *The Country Girl*, in which she played the wife of an alcoholic singer. She was keen to make a screen comeback with Hitchcock's 1964 movie *Marnie*, but the mood in the Principality was against it and the part went to Tippi Hedren.

"The New Brando"

When Warner Bros. signed Paul Newman, they planned to market him as the new Brando. With his smouldering good looks and penetrating blue eyes, Newman undoubtedly had star quality. His first movie, *The Silver Chalice* (1954), was a $40 million disaster, but two years later he had a big hit with *Somebody Up There Likes Me*, based on the life of boxer Rocky Graziano. Newman's portrayal of Brick in *Cat on a Hot Tin Roof* and pool shark Eddie Felson in *The Hustler* both earned him Oscar nominations. The pairing with Robert Redford for *Butch Cassidy and the Sundance Kid*—the highest-grossing western in movie history— helped make Newman the No. 1 box-office star in 1969. The courtroom thriller *The Verdict*, made in 1982, brought him his fifth Oscar nomination.

Right: Newman pictured with Joanne Woodward, whom he married in 1958.

TOUGH GUYS FOUND MOVIE SHRINE

Three of the screen's greatest tough guys got together in 1992 to launch Planet Hollywood, a restaurant that was also a shrine to the movies. The Harley-Davidson ridden by Schwarzenegger in the *Terminator* movies was just one of the exhibits on show. Stallone joined the superstar bracket after insisting that United Artists could only have his screenplay of *Rocky* if they put him in the title role. The studio offered him $150,000 not to play the part. Stallone refused, even though he had just $100 in the bank. Bruce Willis was less demanding when he was plucked from obscurity. *Die Hard*'s John McClane was spotted by a casting director while working as a bartender.

EDWARD G. DEMANDS RICO ROLE

Edward G. Robinson made his name in the 1930 movie *Little Caesar*, in which he played vicious gangster Rico. He refused a minor part in the picture, demanding the lead role, which was clearly inspired by Capone. This wasn't for egotistical reasons; Robinson saw parallels between himself and Rico: both striving to stand out from the herd, though the character had chosen nefarious means of doing so. Producer Hal Wallis pointed out that contractually he was in no position to bargain—before promptly offering him the part with which he would forever be associated.

"BRITAIN'S BAD GIRL"

The teenage Joan Collins had high hopes of becoming a serious stage actress. She went to the Royal Academy of Dramatic Art, where she was a contemporary of David McCallum, but dropped out, choosing hands-on experience with Rank. She appeared in a number of crime thrillers and was dubbed "Britain's Bad Girl." Daryl Zanuck spotted her and signed her to Fox but her Hollywood career never took off. By the 1970s she was best known for a string of horror flicks and TV work, the latter including "Guest Villainess" the siren in the Batman series. Her movie career enjoyed a resurgence with sex romps *The Stud* and *The Bitch*, both penned by sister Jackie. The 1980s brought her most celebrated role, *Dynasty's* Alexis Carrington, which made her queen of the soap opera bitches.

'HERE'S JOHNNY....'

Jack Nicholson spent the first ten years of his career making low-budget movies and deliberately eschewing the Hollywood establishment. His Oscar-nominated performance in *Easy Rider* made him a star, and although it inevitably brought a transition from the alternative to the mainstream, Nicholson remained a singular, stellar talent. He cemented his reputation in movies such as *Five Easy Pieces* and *Chinatown*, then won an Academy Award for his portrayal of Randall P. McMurphy in *One Flew Over The Cuckoo's Nest.* Marlon Brando and Gene Hackman had turned the part down; Nicholson was a free spirit, not interested in pursuing roles which enhanced his image and the perfect anti-hero. It was a bravura performance.

HITCH SETS CORPSE TRAP

Opposite: The Master of Suspense, on the set of *Frenzy.* Hitchcock took the business of scaring people very seriously. When making *Psycho* he left different versions of the mother's corpse around the set for Janet Leigh to stumble upon; he used the pitch of her scream to decide which one to use in the movie.

Right: Sean Connery, the immaculately turned out superspy on the set of *Goldfinger,* his third outing as 007. Established stars including Richard Burton and James Mason were considered for the role of Bond; they would have commanded a substantially higher fee than Connery, who was paid just $15,000.

FORD STARS IN FIRST ROCK 'N' ROLL FILM

Above: Glenn Ford, one of the most popular leading men of the 1950s. *The Big Heat* (1953), in which he played a cop trying to find out who killed his wife, included a scene in which scalding coffee was thrown into a victim's face. It was regarded as a landmark in screen violence.

He tamed delinquent schoolkids in *The Blackboard Jungle*, a movie notable for using "Rock Around the Clock" in the soundtrack.

Opposite: Johnny Depp, Demi Moore and Bruce Willis, pictured at Planet Hollywood.

FORCES' PIN-UP GIRLS

Right: Betty Grable made her screen debut aged 12 and was a seasoned performer in B-movies by 1940, when she got her big break as last-minute replacement for a stricken Alice Faye in *Down Argentine Way*. She was Hollywood's highest paid star for a while, though servicemen were more interested in her legs, insured with Lloyds of London for £250,000.

Opposite: Lana Turner rivaled Betty Grable as the Forces' pin-up girl of World War Two. Fox, RKO and Warner Bros. were unimpressed with her acting ability, but stills of Turner, dubbed "The Sweater Girl", were in great demand and convinced MGM she could be the next great sex symbol. She gave probably her best performance as the femme fatale in the classic noir thriller *The Postman Always Rings Twice*.

OSCAR-WINNING DEBUT FOR HEPBURN

Audrey Hepburn took the movie world by storm in the early 1950s, her enchanting presence leading to comparisons with Garbo and her namesake Katharine. Hepburn had been a chorus girl and bit-part player when she was chosen to star in the Broadway production of *Gigi*. No sooner had she become the darling of the New York theater than William Wyler insisted she play the princess in his forthcoming movie *Roman Holiday*. Co-star Gregory Peck said it was clear from the outset that she would win an Oscar for her performance. The end of the film showed Hepburn was still learning her craft: she couldn't cry on cue as she took her leave of Peck—until an angry Wyler raised his voice. The tears flowed and the cameras rolled. She was Oscar-nominated for her portrayal of Holly Golightly in *Breakfast At Tiffany's*, a part intended for Marilyn Monroe. In 1964 she gave a typically captivating performance as Eliza Dolittle in *My Fair Lady*, a role coveted by Julie Andrews, who had played Eliza in the stage version.

"CAN DANCE A LITTLE..."

Left: Fred Astaire, pictured with his wife Phyllis Potter in 1937. After an early screen test one casting director said of Astaire: "Can't act; slightly bald; can dance a little." He and Ginger Rogers were fourth and fifth in the billing of their first movie together, *Flying Down To Rio*. Their chemistry—and dancing—was sprinkled with stardust and from then on they were the main attraction. At Astaire's insistence the duo could spend weeks perfecting a routine, but made it look magically effortless on screen.

Right: Denzel Washington after he had finished filming the life story of the militant American black activist, *Malcolm X* in 1992. Washington, who played Steve Biko in *Cry Freedom* and the black slave in *Glory,* had waited seven years to play the role.

CASABLANCA'S ALTERNATIVE ENDING

Cary Grant and Ingrid Bergman, co-stars of the 1958 movie *Indiscreet*. Bergman arrived in Hollywood from her native Sweden in 1939 and quickly rose to become Tinseltown's most popular leading lady. Ironically, the picture which made her a stellar name, *Casablanca*, was a chaotic affair. Neither she nor Bogart were keen on the script, which was constantly revised during shooting. Two endings were planned, one had her flying off with husband Paul Henreid, the other staying with Bogey. After shooting the first it was instantly obvious that the alternative would not be required. Bergman won the first of her three Academy Awards for *Gaslight*, playing the woman Charles Boyer was trying to drive insane. Her image was temporarily tarnished when she, a married woman, had a child by director Roberto Rossellini. They later married and Hollywood eventually welcomed her home.

REDFORD TURNS DOWN GRADUATE

Left: With just one successful movie to his credit—playing newlywed husband opposite Jane Fonda in *Barefoot in the Park*—Robert Redford turned down the starring role in *The Graduate*. In 1969 he was teamed with Paul Newman in the phenomenally successful *Butch Cassidy and the Sundance Kid*. The love interest was provided by *Graduate* star Katharine Ross. He went on to link up with the movie's other star, Dustin Hoffmann, in the Watergate conspiracy thriller *All the President's Men*, the rights to which Redford had bought for $425,000. He was Oscar-nominated for his second blockbuster collaboration with Newman, in *The Sting*, but it was as director that he picked up his first major award, for *Ordinary People*.

Opposite: John Travolta studied dance under Fred Kelly—Gene's brother. He became a teen idol with *Saturday Night Fever* and *Grease*. The former was inspired by a magazine article, the latter a Broadway show which had had a lukewarm reception from the critics. Neither movie received good notices: one reviewer thought Travolta would sink without trace for several years following *Grease*. Travolta's career was revitalized after his appearance in Tarantino's *Pulp Fiction*.

A LATE BLOOMER

"I bloomed very early. It's just that no one bothered to notice," was Morgan Freeman's riposte to a comment about his late arrival in Hollywood's hall of fame. And indeed, the Tennessee-born actor had been working on stage, television and in movies for many years before his Oscar-nominated performance in *Driving Miss Daisy* in 1988.

The strong moral presence that is Freeman's trademark can be seen in many of his roles throughout the 90s and early 21st century: Red in the critically acclaimed *The Shawshank Redemption*; the world weary detective in the dark thriller *Seven*; and playing alongside Clint Eastwood in *The Unforgiven* and *Million Dollar Baby*.

In between these high points there have been some less critically successful movies, but Morgan Freeman is always working, with many projects lined up for the future. Now in his late sixties, the late flowering Freeman will be in bloom for many years to come.

CHOOSE BETWEEN GREAT ACTOR AND STAR

With a succession of scintillating stage performances, including *Henry V* (right), Richard Burton was widely seen as one of the greatest talents of the early postwar era. His rich resonant tones delivered Shakespearean lines memorably, but his movie roles were often unworthy of his gifts, particularly in the latter stages of his career. *Cleopatra* (1963) was a case in point. It cost $35 million to make—the most expensive movie in history—but was most notable for Burton's burgeoning love affair with Elizabeth Taylor. Their marriage first-time round ended in 1974, the year in which he made *Il Viaggio* (*The Voyage*) with Sophia Loren (left). Laurence Olivier is said to have told Burton to make up his mind whether he wanted to be a great actor or a star; he was undoubtedly the latter, but most critics agree that his canon did not do justice to his talent.

A NEW BREED OF MALE STAR

Opposite: Roger Moore's dashing looks, silky voice and suave manner made him a natural leading man. Those qualities were well to the fore in his two most famous incarnations, as *The Saint* on TV and as Sean Connery's long-term successor as 007.

Right: By contrast, Michael Caine's Cockney vowels and thick glasses made him a new breed of male star in the 1960s. He served a long apprenticeship in the theater and in minor movie roles, and it was Baker, which earned him a screen test for *Zulu*. He didn't get the part he tested for but impressed enough to be cast as one of the officers. He was nominated for an Oscar for his performance as cheeky Lothario Alfie, and enjoyed huge success as Harry Palmer in three outings as Len Deighton's spy. In neither case was he first choice. Christopher Plummer chose *The Sound Of Music* over *The Ipcress File*, while Laurence Harvey and Terence Stamp were among those who turned *Alfie* down.

TAKING IT ON THE CHIN

Studio bosses initially wanted Kirk Douglas to have the Hollywood's most famous dimpled chin smoothed out with plastic surgery. He oozed virility in the picture which established him as a star, as a boxer in *Champion* (1949). After his Oscar-nominated performance Fox offered him $200,000 for a new project; this was four times the amount the studio could have got him for had they taken up an earlier option. One of his most famous roles, as the prime mover in a slaves' revolt in *Spartacus*, created a storm of protest. The McCarthy witch-hunts were still fresh in the mind and the Cold War temperature was extremely frosty. Dalton Trumbo's script was branded as "Marxian" by one critic, and movie-goers were urged to boycott the picture. The fans saw *Spartacus* as a cracking Roman epic and it eventually did very good business.

AN AMERICAN INSTITUTION

John Wayne was not so much an actor as an institution. He enjoyed enormous popularity from the late 30s through to the 70s; the public knew what they were getting from a "Duke" movie and were rarely disappointed. Interestingly, the one year in which he dipped out of the Top 10 American box office draws, 1958, was the year in which his only picture was an atypical Wayne role, as a diplomat in *The Barbarian and the Geisha*. Riding tall in the saddle in John Ford's *Stagecoach* (1939), or winning the war in the Pacific in *The Sands of Iwo Jima*; these were the kind of roles that were more to the fans' liking. Before *Stagecoach*, his breakthrough movie, Wayne was earning $200 a week. Afterwards, Republic, the minor studio to which he was contracted, was able to loan him out at a weekly rate of $1500. It was for *True Grit* and his portrayal of Rooster Cogburn—a hard-drinking marshal helping Kim Darby avenge her murdered father—that he finally won an Academy Award.

QUEEN OF THE ROMCOM

Opposite: Meg Ryan, pictured at Planet Hollywood for a screening of *Sleepless in Seattle*, the movie which confirmed her reputation as the queen of the romcom. That reputation had been established with *When Harry Met Sally* (1989), whose restaurant scene with Billy Crystal also made her the foremost exponent of the screen orgasm.

Left: Merle Oberon's exotic beauty took the eye of director Alexander Korda, who put her under contract in the late 1920s and later became her husband. She played Anne Boleyn in *The Private Life Of Henry VIII*. Charles Laughton won the Academy Award but Oberon impressed enough for Hollywood to come calling. She recovered from a near-fatal car crash to play Cathy to Olivier's Heathcliff in William Wyler's 1939 adaptation of *Wuthering Heights*. In the 1940s she was groomed as the successor to Bette Davis but her career faded. In the early 50s RKO abandoned four projects and paid up her contract, at a reputed cost of $800,000.

VADIM'S NEW PROTÉGÉ

Opposite: With Roger Vadim as her mentor, Catherine Deneuve unsurprisingly was given roles which traded on her enormous sex appeal. She starred in Polanski's *Repulsion* (1965) as an inhibited girl driven to insanity and murder living in a large London house. Her biggest success came in *Belle De Jour*, in which she played a middle-class housewife who turns to prostitution as an entertaining diversion.

Above: Dean Martin went solo after a long career as Jerry Lewis' straight man. He starred in a couple of good John Wayne westerns and was Matt Helm, America's answer to James Bond. His "Rat Pack" romps, *Oceans 11* and *Robin And The Seven Hoods*, were among his most popular movies.

$7 MILLION FOR CLEOPATRA

Enid Bagnold's story about a girl who trains her horse to ride in the Grand National was mooted as a vehicle for Katharine Hepburn, Vivien Leigh and Shirley Temple before it made a star of 12-year-old Elizabeth Taylor. By the age of 18 the close attention of the studio system and an ambitious mother had left her eager to marry. She became close to Montgomery Clift during the making of *A Place In The Sun*, but he was 12 years her senior—and homosexual. During shooting she met Nicky Hilton, a member of the hotelier family. Without a trace of irony she said their relationship would endure "because we both adore oversize sweaters, hamburgers with onions and Ezio Pinza." A more perspicacious studio boss noted: "He'll make a very nice first husband." Taylor was on her fourth marriage—to Eddie Fisher—when she met Richard Burton on the set of *Cleopatra*. Her $125,000 fee, $3000 a week expenses, $5000 for each week's overrun (it did, massively) and 10 percent of the gross brought her some $7 million in total. President Kennedy's annual salary at the time was $150,000.

SWANSON'S FINANCIAL BLACK HOLE

Opposite: Gloria Swanson, pictured with daughter Michelle in 1950. Swanson worked with two of the great film makers of the silent era: Mack Sennett and Cecil B. DeMille. By the early 1920s her name went above the title of her movies and she could just about name her terms to Paramount. Eventually she chose artistic freedom above money, rejecting $18,000 a week to move to United Artists. Much of her vast wealth disappeared in one ill-fated project: *Queen Kelly*. The story of a convent girl who undergoes a number of trials before inheriting a fortune became a financial black hole in the hands of extravagant director Erich von Stroheim. The project was over $500,000 in the red when Swanson fired him. The picture was completed but had a limited release, making it one of the great commercial disasters in movie history. It took Swanson years to recover from the losses incurred.

Right: Acting rescued Gerard Depardieu from a delinquent childhood. The man dubbed "France's de Niro" received an Oscar nomination for his performance in *Cyrano De Bergerac* (1990), the movie which launched his Hollywood career.

THE BENCHMARK FOR ALL ACTRESSES

"Garbo Talks!" ran the strap-line for *Anna Christie*, the 1930 movie in which the silent screen star's voice was heard for the first time. Some actors failed to make the transition, notably John Gilbert, who had been the envy of men the world over as Garbo's screen lover on several occasions in the silent era. But with the arrival of talkies Garbo merely confirmed her status as the greatest screen actress of them all, and by common consent the most beautiful. Giving interviews was not her forte, however, and when a friend coined the phrase "I want to be alone" to prevent her from having to endure that chore it simply added to the mystique and allure. There was certainly no socialising going to and from the MGM lot: a limousine took her back and forth to her accommodation—a distance of 20 yards. Garbo turned her back on Hollywood after making *Two-Faced Woman* in 1941. She was 36.

DISGRUNTLED LOAN STAR WINS OSCAR

Left: French-born actress Claudette Colbert excelled at playing women with impish charm in the 1930s. The roles were wide-ranging but her forte was undoubtedly for comedy.

Opposite: The famous hitchhiking scene from the 1934 Frank Capra movie *It Happened One Night*, in which Colbert plays a runaway heiress who falls for unemployed hack Clark Gable. Her raised skirt eventually wins out over Gable's thumbing technique. Neither star wanted to do the movie and were unimpressed with the script. Both had been loaned to Columbia—Colbert from Paramount, Gable from MGM—as punishment for their lack of co-operation over other projects. It became a comedy classic, sweeping the board at the Oscars. Legend has it that Colbert was at the railway station when she should have been picking up her Best Actress award, believing she had no chance of winning.

NO TEARS FOR NIVEN

David Niven, pictured opposite after his 1948 marriage to Hjordis Tersmesden (his first wife died earlier that year, after falling down a flight of stairs at a party). Niven had walk-on parts and one-liners before *The Charge of the Light Brigade* (1936). He and the movie's star Errol Flynn became great friends, the two celebrated roisterers sharing a house together for a while. *Wuthering Heights* (1939) showed how Niven's bargaining power had increased in three years. When his character, Edgar Linton, was required to shed tears, he informed director William Wyler that his contract stated that he wouldn't be asked to cry. Wyler solved the problem by asking him to bury his face instead.

HOLLYWOOD'S GOLDEN COUPLE

Opposite: Clark Gable and Carole Lombard in a scene from *No Man of Her Own* (1933). Lombard learned her comic timing working with Mack Sennett in the 1920s. During the following decade she used her talents to good effect in a number of memorable screwball comedies. *Mr. And Mrs. Smith*, in which she and husband Robert Montgomery discover they aren't really married, was directed by Hitchcock; his adoration for the actress prompted the departure from his usual genre. Lombard was briefly married to William Powell; in 1939 she and Gable wed, becoming Hollywood's golden couple. She was killed in a plane crash in 1942, aged 34.

Right: The King of Hollywood. In the 1930s Clark Gable was at the forefront of a new breed of leading men, who jousted with women rather than just simpered in their presence. The rough edge and twinkling eye—even the jug ears—were box office gold dust, his manliness appealing to male movie-goers too. After his Oscar-winning performance in *It Happened One Night* undershirt sales plummeted because Gable appeared on screen without one. He was not keen to play Rhett Butler in *Gone With the Wind;* contractual agreements forced him to accept his most famous role.

ROWDY TO THE MAN WITH NO NAME

The poncho-wearing, cheroot-chewing models depict the character which catapulted Clint Eastwood from TV actor to world star. He had already done six seasons as Rowdy Yates in *Rawhide* when he first played The Man With No Name, in *A Fistful of Dollars*. "Spaghetti Western" entered the language, although the Sergio Leone movie was shot in Spain, on a budget of just $200,000. Eastwood's fee was $15,000; by the third in the series, *The Good, The Bad and The Ugly*, he commanded $250,000 plus a percentage. By 1972, when his portrayal of uncompromising cop Harry Callahan first hit the screens, he was No. 1 at the box office. He only got the role after original choice Frank Sinatra suffered a sprained wrist.

WINNING SMILE

Julia Roberts received an an Oscar nomination, as well as being catapulted to super stardom, for her role in the aptly titled *Pretty Woman.* This established her as the world's favorite romantic comedy actress and the hottest property in Hollywood who, 15 years on, can command $20 million for a movie. Modestly Roberts says "I'm just an ordinary person who has an extraordinary job."

Opposite: Julia Roberts arrives at the world premiere of *Mona Lisa Smile* at New York's Ziegfeld Theater in December 2003.

FLYNN INHERITS FAIRBANKS' MANTLE

Errol Flynn (pictured opposite with his third wife Patrice Wymore) took over from Douglas Fairbanks Sr. as the movie's great swashbuckling hero. His breakthrough came in 1935, when he inherited the lead in *Captain Blood*, a role intended for Robert Donat. In an earlier movie that year he had been 11th in the billing; now he was a star. *The Charge of the Light Brigade* and *The Adventures of Robin Hood* provided classic vehicles for his dashing screen persona. In 1939 he co-starred with Bette Davis in *The Private Lives of Elizabeth and Essex*. Originally called *Elizabeth the Queen*, it was changed as Flynn's contract stipulated that the title had to make reference to him.

VALIANT MATRIARCH MARRIES "SON"

Right: Greer Garson was signed to MGM after Louis B. Mayer saw her in a West End play in 1938. Her first Hollywood role was wife to Robert Donat in *Goodbye Mr. Chips*. At 31 she was too old to play the temptress; but during the war years she was the archetypal indomitable matriarch, the perfect role model to women whose families were ravaged by the conflict. The apogee came in the 1942 picture *Mrs. Miniver*, for which she won the Best Actress award. A year later she married Richard Ney, who had played her son in the movie. The studio asked for a judicious delay in their nuptials while the picture did the rounds at the box office.

Opposite: Gary Cooper's image was mild-mannered, diffident even, but with a simmering virility never far below the surface. In his two Oscar-winning performances, for *Sergeant York* and *High Noon,* Cooper played the meek guy stirred to action. It was a quality the actor felt resonated with middle America and helped maintain his popularity for 30 years.

SWASHBUCKLING RIVALRY

Opposite: Tony Curtis and Kirk Douglas, pictured with Douglas's second wife Anne Buydens. The two were making *The Vikings*, one of the hit movies of 1958, and were reunited two years later for *Spartacus*. Burt Lancaster was the other great swashbuckling star of the 1950s. He co-starred with Curtis in *Trapeze* (1956) and featured with Douglas in several pictures, including *Gunfight at the OK Corral*. Douglas saw Lancaster as his arch-rival and was relieved when he felt that he'd finally emerged from Lancaster's shadow.

Right: Ewan McGregor, star of *Trainspotting* and *Moulin Rouge!* arrives at a Unicef charity auction in London October 2004. He had recently completed a trip from London to New York "The Wrong Way" by riding a motorbike east, via Europe, Asia, Alaska and Canada. The motorbike he traveled on with fellow actor Charlie Boorman was being auctioned for the charity.

HITCHCOCK ROLE FOR CALAMITY JANE

Doris Day and James Stewart, who starred in Hitchcock's *The Man Who Knew Too Much*, a stylish 1956 version of a picture the director had originally made 22 years earlier. It was Stewart's third collaboration with Hitchcock, following *Rope* and *Rear Window*. *Vertigo* would follow two years later, confirming him as one of Hitchcock's favorite leading men. For Doris Day, who rose to become America's No.1 box office star on the strength of musicals such as *Calamity Jane*, the movie showed her dramatic range. Even Hitchcock wasn't about to let her musical talents go to waste, however, and the storyline incorporated the song "Que Sera Sera," which won an Oscar.

OSCAR FOR 77-YEAR-OLD FONDA

Henry Fonda received his first Oscar nomination for *The Grapes of Wrath* (1940), the story of a family struggling for survival in the dustbowl of the Depression era. It was a classic Fonda role: solid, dependable, sincere. Like Gary Cooper, Fonda was slow to rouse but always ready to make a stand when the chips were down. In *Twelve Angry Men* (1956) he stuck to his principles in a taut jury-room drama. It wasn't a box-office hit but the critics acclaimed it and Fonda himself regarded it as his finest work. His career spanned almost 50 years, yet it was not until 1982, the year of his death, that he finally won the Best Actor award, for *On Golden Pond*.

GOING SOLO

Four years after his performance as Bob Falfa in *American Graffiti*, Harrison Ford shot to fame for his role as Han Solo in *Star Wars*. From that time he has established himself as a Hollywood giant with starring roles in four of the ten highest-grossing movies of all time. Roles such as Jack Ryan, created by Tom Clancy, and Indiana Jones added to his stardom. He received Golden Globe nominations for powerful roles as John Book in *Witness* and as Dr. Richard Kimble in *The Fugitive*.

Right: Making a speech in London in 1993 while promoting *The Fugitive*. Ford was sealing a time capsule at the new Warner West End movie theater complex containing a message for the people of 2093.

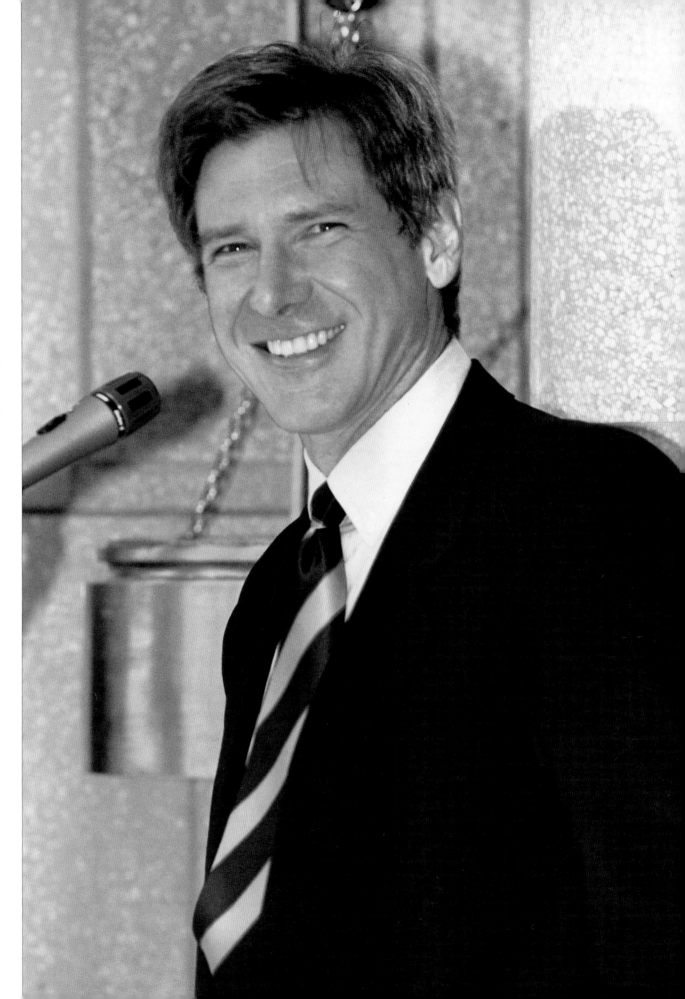

FROM FLOP TO CLASSIC

It's A Wonderful Life figures in many people's list of greatest all-time movies. The story of a man who wishes he'd never been born, only to be shown the consequences by an ageing guardian angel, was Stewart's personal favorite, though it made no money on release and precipitated the swift demise of Liberty Pictures. He received one of his five Oscar nominations for his performance in the movie Mr. Smith Goes To Washington, in which he played a senator fighting against the system, a typical Stewart role, brought him another. For his big filibustering speech director Frank Capra said his supposed sore throat wasn't coming across. Stewart consulted an ENT specialist, who duly proffered a chemical to do the trick. The Philadelphia Story (1940) gave Stewart his only Oscar in a career spanning 50 years.

AN ALIEN IN NEW YORK

Opposite: Sigourney Weaver at the Bafta Awards in London, 1994. The daughter of a British actress, and a father who was a producer, Susan Alexandra Weaver was born in New York City. When she was just 15 Susan changed her name to Sigourney, after the character Sigourney Howard, in Fitzgerald's *The Great Gatsby*. Following a successful stage career she played the part of the tough, uncompromising Ripley in *Alien* in 1977 which made her an overnight star.

Right: Twenty-two-year-old Judi Dench rehearsing the part of Ophelia in *Hamlet* at London's Old Vic.

"LA LOLLO"

In the 1950s Gina Lollobrigida rivaled Sophia Loren as Italy's most popular actress—and greatest—sex symbol. "La Lollo" had a long track record in European cinema when she was chosen to play Bogie's voluptuous wife in *Beat The Devil*. With John Huston directing it should have been a sure-fire hit but it sat uneasily between comedy and drama. "In glorious black and white" ran the ads, but the joke backfired; audiences didn't like it and one theater owner refunded the admission money. In *Trapeze* (1956), Lollobrigida's first American blockbuster, she was the love interest that came between Tony Curtis and Burt Lancaster. It was set in France for a particular reason: a contractual wrangle with Howard Hughes and RKO prevented her from filming in the US. For the same reason the 1959 biblical epic *Solomon and Sheba* was shot in Spain. MGM finally bought out her existing contract and she made movies through to the early 70s but La Lollo remained a bigger star in Europe than Hollywood.

COMIC STRIP

Left: Edward Regen Murphy found fame at a young age. Born April 3 1961, in Brooklyn, his comic talents manifested themselves in junior high where he would entertain his fellow students at New York's Roosevelt High School. From the age of 15 he was earning money from his stock of gags, monologues and impersonations in stand-up in local halls and bars. He progressed to the famous Comic Strip, and at just 19 was offered a role in NBC's *Saturday Night Live*.

Already a big name in the US, Eddie Murphy shot to worldwide fame in 1982 when he was cast as convict Reggie Hammond, temporarily teamed up with Nick Nolte's hard nosed cop, in *48 Hours*. Since this high profile debut, movies have been Murphy's metier, with numerous memorable parts. In the 80s roles as Axel Foley in the *Beverley Hills Cop* movies and the wise-talking conman in *Trading Places* established his name.

Disappointing movies in the late 80s and early 90s, including his directorial debut *Harlem Nights*, in which he directed his comedy hero Richard Pryor, marked difficult times and turmoil in his private life. But a remake of *The Nutty Professor* in 1996 brought a new phase of more family oriented pictures, including providing the voices for animated films, most famously the wise-cracking donkey in *Shrek*.

Opposite: Brother of Shirley MacLaine, Warren Beatty was groomed for stardom at an early age playing prominent roles in television and theater before reaching the big screen. After playing minor parts in the early sixties he graduated to become producer and star of the highly successful *Bonnie and Clyde* in 1967. In 1975 he wrote his first screenplay, *Shampoo* and then directed *Heaven Can Wait* in 1978. In 1981 he produced, directed, co-scripted and acted in *Reds*, earning him an Oscar for Best Director.

THE ZEITGEIST ACTRESS

Perhaps more than any other actress Julie Christie (pictured right rehearsing for *Oh Calcutta!* with Jane Birkin and Gabrielle Crawford) captured the 60s zeitgeist. In only her third film, *Billy Liar*, she played the free spirit who provided Tom Courtenay with a much needed escape route from the drudgery of clerical work and family life. Christie was excellent, though the makers of *Darling* initially thought her too inexperienced to star in the 1965 movie about a good-time girl. The money men made a wise choice; Christie won an Oscar. She was nominated for her role in *McCabe and Mrs. Miller* (1971), one of three movies she made with real-life partner Warren Beatty. The third, *Heaven Can Wait*, was a remake of the 1941 picture *Here Comes Mr. Jordan*. In the original it was a boxer who dies and is allowed to return to earth, only to find his body has been cremated. In the remake Beatty played a football player who suffers the same fate.

OSCAR FOR LEFT-WING FIREBRAND

Vanessa Redgrave became as well known for her left-wing activism as her acting. A member of a famous dynasty of thespians, Redgrave was one of the brightest talents of the British theater in the early 1960s before effortlessly turning her talents to film. She was nominated for an Oscar for only her second movie, *A Suitable Case For Treatment,* in which she played the wife to David Warner's Morgan. There were two more nominations before she picked up the Best Supporting Actress award for Fred Zinnemann's *Julia.* Redgrave played the title role, a woman who disappeared in Nazi Germany. Lillian Hellmann, played by Jane Fonda, reflects on her friend's fate. This was poetic license at work, as the two never met. They shared the same lawyer and it was he who told Hellmann Julia's story. Inevitably, Redgrave used the platform of the Oscars to make a political point. Her pro-Palestinian remarks almost resulted in her being sacked from her latest project, *Yanks,* but director John Schlesinger interceded, insisting that she was being employed for her acting ability, not her political views.

MAN IN BLACK

Right: Music was Will Smith's first love. *The Fresh Prince of Bel Air*—the TV sitcom which launched his acting career—took its title from his rap artist name. Before the show ended its six-year run Smith had broken into movies with *Six Degrees Of Separation*, playing the mysterious Paul, who enters the life of Donald Sutherland and Stockard Channing claiming to be a friend of their son. *Independence Day* and *Men in Black* were huge hits, and Smith joined the $20 million-a-movie set with his brilliant portrayal of the boxing legend in *Ali*, a role which earned him an Oscar nomination.

Opposite: Leonardo DiCaprio made his TV debut aged five. He quickly set his sights on an acting career, and after years of appearing in commercials and educational films he took the lead in the coming-of-age movie *This Boy's Life*. His ill-fated love affair with Kate Winslett in the multi-Oscar-winning *Titanic* elevated him to the superstar bracket. Success has allowed DiCaprio the freedom to choose diverse, challenging roles, such as the mentally handicapped teenager in *What's Eating Gilbert Grape* and obsessive billionaire Howard Hughes in *The Aviator*.

I COULD'VE BEEN A CONTENDER...

Above: Marlon Brando, pictured with Sophia Loren in 1954, the year in which he won his first Oscar for *On The Waterfront*. Many thought he should have won for his electrifying performance as Kowalski in *A Streetcar Named Desire* (1951). Vivien Leigh, Karl Malden and Kim Hunter, who like Brando were reprising their stage roles, all won Oscars; Brando lost out to Bogart, who was named Best Actor for *The African Queen*.

Opposite: Sean Connery meets Pussy Galore in *Goldfinger*, his third outing as 007. *The Longest Day*—the last movie he made before *Dr. No* launched him to superstardom—had such a stellar cast that Connery didn't make it into the top 20 in the billing.

BARBRA BRINGS BRICE TO BIG SCREEN

Barbra Streisand was a very successful stage performer and singer but a novice movie actor when she was handed the lead role in *Funny Girl*. She had wowed theater-goers in New York and London in the role of Fanny Brice, but it still represented a gamble. Contracts were already signed for two more movies, *Hello Dolly* and *On A Clear Day You Can See Forever*, so the investment in Streisand's undoubted talent was huge. It paid off with *Funny Girl* one of the smash hits of 1968. The movie told the true story of Fanny Brice, a gauche Jewish comedienne from New York who becomes a Broadway star. There were obvious parallels between the two, although unlike Brice, Streisand did make the transition from stage to movie star. Streisand reprised her Oscar-winning role seven years later in *Funny Lady*. It wasn't a roaring success but it did give Streisand an Oscar for the song 'Evergreen'.

OUTSTANDING NEWCOMER

Jude Law started acting with the National Youth Music Theatre at the age of 12. He began his stage career when he was 20 and was nominated for the Olivier Award of "Outstanding Newcomer" before achieving similar success in America. His first big break on the screen was in *Gattaca* with Uma Thurman in 1997. Law became well established as a star two years later following his performance in *The Talented Mr. Ripley*.

Left: Law with Eve Best who starred in the Jacobean tragedy, *'Tis Pity She's A Whore*, at the Young Vic in 1999.

Right: With girlfriend Sienna Miller at Wimbledon watching Tim Henman's quarter final encounter in 2004.

WHAT'S IT ALL ABOUT, ALFIE...

Three movies in as many years turned Michael Caine from an actor for whom you would have to search a long way down the bill to an international star. Pictured left in 1963, the year in which he earned excellent reviews for his role in *Zulu*, Caine next appeared in *The Ipcress File* as Harry Palmer, the gadget-free antidote to Bond who would be seen supermarket shopping and cooking when not unearthing a mole. But it was the 1966 film *Alfie* which took Caine (pictured right at the film's premiere) into a new league. He had inherited the role of Palmer from Christopher Plummer, and several leading actors had turned down the lead in the film version of Bill Naughton's play. Made for a paltry $500,000, *Alfie* not only did excellent business for Paramount in Britain but also successfully crossed the Atlantic. In 1972 Caine brought another play to the screen and showed how far he'd come as an actor. Anthony Shaffer's ingenious thriller *Sleuth* had just two actors playing the three characters. Caine played two of them, Laurence Olivier one, in a movie which earned both Oscar nominations.

THE TRAMP

When Charlie Chaplin joined Mack Sennett's Keystone, he found a studio that had a fixed idea about comedy—notably that the climax always featured a chase. Chaplin, who preferred comic ideas to develop from character, was something of a marginal figure until he was asked to provide some impromptu comedy business to fill a scene. He went to the props room and extemporized the character of The Tramp, creating great mirth on the set. Sennett eventually relented, although Chaplin later discovered this wasn't merely a change of heart over what was funny and what wasn't; he'd had a huge increase in demand for prints of Chaplin pictures. He left Keystone to join Essanay in 1914, his salary jumping from $175 to $1250 a week. London-born Chaplin, pictured opposite with Winston Churchill and above with his adoring fans, was awarded special Oscars in 1928 and 1972, and knighted in 1975.

GENE AND JERRY

Opposite: Gene Kelly needed little encouragement to accept an *Invitation to the Dance* (1955). Both Kelly's career and the era of the great Hollywood musical were in their final throes, but in the previous fifteen years he had starred in a host of Hollywood classics, including *On the Town*, *Anchors Aweigh*, *An American in Paris* and, unforgettably, *Singin' In The Rain*. *Sailors on Furlough* was a stock plot device, but that mattered little. His dancing—more athletic than Astaire's—was a joy, his choreography innovative. A dazzling sequence involving the cartoon Jerry Mouse in *Anchors Aweigh* helped to earn him an Oscar nomination. *An American in Paris* (1951) won a string of Oscars, including Best Picture. It featured a remarkable 20-minute ballet sequence which cost over $500,000 to make, for which the Academy gave Kelly a long-overdue special Oscar.

Left: Halle Berry first came to public attention at just 17 years of age when she won the Miss Teen All-American Pageant in 1985. In the early 90s 30 million viewers across America tuned in to watch her portray the author Alex Haley's late grandmother in *Queen*, the final part of the *Roots* saga. Berry reached an even wider audience when she became the only official Bond Girl to win an Academy Award when she played alongside Pierce Brosnan in *Die Another Day*.

HOOFER TURNS GANGSTER

Right: James Cagney (pictured right
on the set of the 1959 movie *Never
Steal Anything Small*) established
himself as the archetypal screen tough
in *The Public Enemy*. He was originally
cast as the good guy, director William
Wellmann switching his role with that
of co-star Eddie Woods at the last
minute. The famous scene in which
he ground half a grapefruit into Mae
Clarke's face was based on a real
incident: a Chicago gangster had
done the same thing to a garrulous
girlfriend, except that he used an
omelette. Although he will forever be
associated with his gangster movies,
Cagney started out as a "hoofer." It
was a return to his musical roots,
playing George M. Cohan in *Yankee
Doodle Dandy*, which brought him his
only Oscar.

Opposite: Stan Laurel and Oliver Hardy
had both been in the business for
some time before Hal Roach decided
to make a comic team of them in
1927. Stan was the driving force and
more inventive of the two, the reverse
of their screen personae.

OLD-FASHIONED ALLURE

Left: Raquel Welch clad in a prehistoric bikini in *One Million Years BC* was one of the enduring images of the 1960s. The role had been intended for Ursula Andress — who four years earlier had so memorably emerged from the surf in *Dr. No*—but when the Swiss-born actress refused, it paved the way for Welch to be heralded as America's new sex goddess. Her subsequent pictures were invariably flimsy, and it was her physical appearance rather than her acting which caused a stir. Welch's first meaty role came in *Myra Breckenridge*, based on a Gore Vidal novel. In it she was teamed with a sex symbol of a bygone era, Mae West, who took the honors both on and off the screen.

Opposite: Brad Pitt and fellow actor Henry Thomas. In just 13 years Brad Pitt went from earning just $6000 for his cameo role as J. D. in *Thelma and Louise* to more than $17 million for the lead in the 2004 blockbuster *Troy*.

O'TOOLE STARS IN LEAN EPIC

Opposite: Rising star Peter O'Toole, pictured in 1959. He had been acclaimed for his stage credits, which included playing Jimmy Porter in Osborne's *Look Back In Anger*, and was about to break into movies with Disney's *Kidnapped*.

Right: O'Toole with wife Sian Phillips at the premiere of *The Day They Robbed the Bank of England* (1960), an entertaining period heist caper. He spent much of 1961 working in the theater before being catapulted into the media spotlight in the lead role in David Lean's historical epic *Lawrence of Arabia*. After Albert Finney turned the part down, Lean and producer Sam Spiegel decided to look for a British actor whose dynamism and charisma would compensate for a lack of international reputation. Visually stunning, *Lawrence of Arabia* was a big hit both with the critics and audiences, despite a running time of nearly four hours.

STONE GIVES BREAK TO MAXIMUS

Above: Sharon Stone is said to have recruited Russell Crowe for
The Quick And The Dead after hearing of his performance in the 1992
Australian movie *Romper Stomper*. Crowe's rise continued with the
stylish *LA Confidential* before going into orbit as the vengeful Maximus
in *Gladiator*.

Opposite: Early in his acting career Welsh-born Reginald Truscott-Jones
made the wise decision to change his name—to Ray Milland. He had
been a stalwart leading man for some 15 years when Billy Wilder
elicited his finest performance, as an alcoholic in *The Lost Weekend*.
After a quarter of a century of wearing a toupée, Milland finally
revealed his bald pate to the world as Ryan O'Neal's father in
Love Story.

MATINÉE IDOL

With his matinée idol looks, beefcake physique and engaging personality, Rock Hudson had the wherewithal for a fine acting career. George Stevens handed him his big break by casting him in the lead role in *Giant*, which became the biggest-grossing movie of 1956. Both he and co-star James Dean were Oscar-nominated for their performances. Despite his he-man image, Hudson's greatest successes came in romantic comedies. In 1959 he made *Pillow Talk*, the first of several collaborations with Doris Day which were extremely popular with the fans. With the studios' connivance Hudson dated a succession of women to perpetuate his red-blooded image.

Opposite: Hudson and his wife Phyllis Gates in 1956.

SCREEN HEAVY TOPS THE POP CHARTS

Left: Lee Marvin had the perfect physiognomy for menace, and used it to good effect in a number of 1950s thrillers. He was the heavy who threw boiling coffee in Gloria Grahame's face in Fritz Lang's *The Big Heat* (1953), a typical Marvin role. However, it is for a spoof western and a musical that he is probably best remembered. He gave an Oscar-winning performance as a drunken gunslinger trying to help out Jane Fonda in *Cat Ballou* (1965); and four years later he starred with Clint Eastwood in Lerner and Loewe's *Paint Your Wagon*, the most unlikely pairing ever seen in a screen musical. It also made Marvin an even more unlikely pop star as his big production number "*Wand'rin' Star*" went to the top of the charts.

Opposite: Anthony Quinn (left) with Frank Sinatra in 1969. Having appeared in more movies with other Oscar-winning actors than any other Oscar-winning actor—a total of 46 in all, Quinn will probably be best remembered for his starring role in the 1964 movie *Zorba the Greek*.

BRYNNER'S FIVE-YEAR REIGN

Opposite: Yul Brynner, pictured with Sheila Rosin during the making of *The Battle Of Neretva*, a Yugoslavian-made war spectacular which won the Academy Award for the best foreign film of 1969. Brynner shaved his hair for the role of the King of Siam in the Broadway version of *The King and I*. He remained hairless for the screen version in 1956, by which time he had been playing the part for five years. It won him the Academy Award, and the same year also saw the long-awaited release of DeMille's epic *The Ten Commandments*, in which Brynner played the Pharaoh. While Brynner was in the middle of his stage run as the King, Akira Kurosawa made *Seven Samurai*, a movie about 16th century Japanese villagers under siege who enlist the help of samurai warriors. This would be the template for John Sturges' classic western, *The Magnificent Seven*, which gave Brynner his other most memorable screen role.

Right: Zsa Zsa Gabor was a former Miss Hungary who was better known for her appearances in the society pages than her movies, although she did feature in Orson Welles' 1958 classic *Touch Of Evil*.

GIANT REBEL

Opposite: James Dean's Adonis-like looks and passionate intensity made him a screen icon; his death at 24 elevated him to cult status. Dean was often compared with Brando, and it was Elia Kazan—who directed Brando in *A Streetcar Named Desire* —who saw Dean on stage and cast him as Cal in *East Of Eden*. His fee was just $18,000. There was more teenage angst in *Rebel Without a Cause*, and in his final movie, *Giant*, he showed his range by ageing with his character in Edna Ferber's sprawling Texan saga. Dean crashed his Porsche the day after shooting was completed. He had already been penciled in for for several roles, including *Somebody Up There Likes Me*.

Left: In 1995 Tom Hanks equaled Spencer Tracy's record of almost six decades earlier by winning successive Best Actor Oscars. He won that year's award for *Forrest Gump*, following his 1994 success for playing an AIDS victim in *Philadelphia*. Tracy won in 1937 and 1938, for *Captains Courageous* and *Boys' Town* respectively.

MAGNETIC APPEAL

Right: The machismo Steve McQueen brought to the screen in movies such as *Bullitt* and *The Magnificent Seven* was no act. The famous motorcycle sequence in *The Great Escape* was included at his request and McQueen himself did all the riding. The only exception was a 50ft jump across a border fence: he crashed during the attempt and a stunt double was brought in. It was from two wheels to four in *Bullitt*, a picture which featured one of the greatest car chases in movie history. Warner Bros. panicked when costs escalated to over $5 million. The studio shouldn't have worried; McQueen's magnetic appeal ensured it recouped three times that figure on release.

Opposite: Sean Penn's father, Leo, was one of Hollywood's blacklisted actors in the McCarthy era. Penn Jr. emerged as one of the brightest new acting talents in the mid-1980s. In the early days his performances tended to be overshadowed by his volatile behavior, not to mention his four-year marriage to Madonna. But the 1990s saw him develop into one of most accomplished actors of his generation. His performance as a retarded father fighting for custody of his daughter in *I Am Sam* (2001) was a triumph, bringing him yet another Oscar nomination.

FULL OF SUSPENSE

Above: Grace Kelly gave a fine performance as the long-suffering wife of dipsomaniac husband Bing Crosby in *The Country Girl*, though with hindsight most commentators felt she was fortunate to win the Best Actress Oscar. Against outstanding opposition—notably Judy Garland in *A Star Is Born*—the Academy appeared to get carried along on a tide of enthusiasm for Hollywood's golden girl, as indeed the public did. Hitchcock preferred Kelly's latent sexuality to the overt smouldering of a Monroe. He felt that sex—just like a good thriller—was all the better for having a degree of suspense.

Opposite: Kelly met Prince Rainier during the making of *To Catch a Thief*, her third Hitchcock movie. After making two more pictures she retired to take up her permanent role as Princess Grace of Monaco. It left George Stevens needing to find a new female lead for *Giant*, Elizabeth Taylor eventually inheriting Kelly's role in the Texan saga.

NO LOCKWOOD DÉCOLLETAGE FOR AMERICA

Right: Bob Hope, pictured with Margaret Lockwood, Britain's most popular actress of the 1940s—and possessor of the most famous beauty spot in show business. The pinnacle of Lockwood's pre-war career came in Hitchcock's *The Lady Vanishes* (1938), in which she and Michael Redgrave set out to discover why the nice grandmotherly Miss Froy has disappeared in mid-train journey. Lockwood—like Hitchcock—went to Hollywood soon afterward, but while the Master of Suspense triumphed with *Rebecca*, Lockwood was soon on her way home. Her popularity in Britain soared to new heights with *The Man In Grey* and *The Wicked Lady*, in both of which she played the scheming villainess. In the latter she did a sideline in highway robbery; she also wore Regency costume which displayed a fine décolletage. This was too revealing for American tastes and the picture had to be reshot with more modest apparel for that market. Even Lockwood tired of the 'devious sinner' roles but as the parts got no better and her popularity waned. She left the movie scene to pursue a stage career.

HESTON EPICS COMBAT TV THREAT

Right: Charlton Heston, pictured at the premiere of *The Big Country* (1959). One way in which Hollywood responded to the threat posed by television was to make blockbuster sagas with dramatic backdrops. 3-D was another. Heston appeared in a number of epic productions, notably The *Ten Commandments* and *Ben Hur*. In the former a baby son was born to the Hestons just in time to play baby Moses, father playing the adult character. He won an Oscar for *Ben Hur*, which also won the Best Picture category. Neither movie earned much praise from the critics but they were huge hits with the fans, the latter credited with saving MGM. The theory of combating TV with lavish screen spectacles was vindicated, temporarily at least.

Opposite: Samuel L. Jackson arrives at the premiere of Paramount's *Coach Carter* at the Chinese Theater, Los Angeles, in January 2005. Jackson played bad guys before becoming an action hero in *Die Hard: With A Vengeance*. But it was his performance in *Pulp Fiction* that gave him an Oscar nomination for his role as Jules Winnfield.

EASY RIDER

Opposite: Henry Fonda once noted that his son Peter made *Easy Rider* for $400,000, and the $40 million it took at the box office eclipsed his own entire career earnings. The cult movie spawned one cult actor: not Fonda or Dennis Hopper but the small-town lawyer who joins their fruitless search to find America. Serendipity played a part in Jack Nicholson's breakthrough picture: he'd been due to play C. W. Moss in *Bonnie And Clyde* but it was decided he resembled Warren Beatty too much and the role went to Michael J. Pollard. That freed him at exactly the moment when Rip Torn pulled out of *Easy Rider*. Nicholson had worked with both Fonda and Hopper before and was quickly recruited to the cast of the classic road movie.

Left: Mel Gibson on a visit to Planet Hollywood in London. Mel Gibson initially made his name in 1979 in Australia where he took the lead role for the first of the three *Mad Max* movies. In 1987, stardom beckoned when he portrayed the homicide cop, Martin Riggs, in *Lethal Weapon*; two equally successful sequels then followed. He made his directorial debut with *Man Without a Face* in 1993 but is best remembered for directing and playing the leading role as William Wallace in *Braveheart* in 1995. This explosive historical action movie earned Best Director and Best Picture at the Golden Globe Awards.

THEATRICAL KNIGHT MEETS SEX SYMBOL

Right: Laurence Olivier, widely regarded as the greatest Sheakespearean actor ever, seen here playing Hamlet. In one Old Vic season, 1937-38, as well as playing the Prince of Denmark Olivier took the stage as Henry V, Coriolanus, Macbeth and Iago. His screen versions of *Henry V* (1944), *Hamlet* (1948) and *Richard III* (1955) became instant classics. It took Olivier time to adapt to movies. He was one of several actors who tried out for *Queen Christina* (1933), playing opposite Garbo. She was unimpressed, and Olivier admitted "I couldn't hold a candle to her." Six years later, playing Heathcliff in *Wuthering Heights*, director William Wyler picked him up for making too many grand theatrical gestures. He heeded the advice and turned in a mesmerizing performance which earned him one of his eight Oscar nominations.

Opposite: The knight of the theater co-starred with the ultimate sex goddess in *The Prince And The Showgirl* (1958). Chorus girl Monroe took the lion's share of the money; Olivier, who also directed, turned in his usual consummate performance as the Ruritanian prince, but the movie failed to live up to its billing.

OF STAGE AND SCREEN

Left: Kevin Spacey's career in movies began with a small part as a thief in *Heartburn* in 1986 but it was with a bigger role as an office manager in *Glengarry Glen Ross* in 1992 that he became well known. Three years later, it was his part as Verbal Kint in acclaimed *The Usual Suspects* that launched him into stardom with an Oscar for Best Supporting Actor. But Spacey likes to stay out of the public eye as he explained in an interview in the *London Evening Standard*: "It's not that I want to create some mystique by maintaining a silence about my personal life, it is just that the less you know about me, the easier it is to convince you that I am that character on screen. It allows an audience to come into a movie theater and believe I am that person." As one of the most distinguished stage actors there was no surprise when, in 1999, he scooped the Oscar for Best Actor for his part as the dark and complex Lester Burnham in *American Beauty.*

Opposite: Marilyn Monroe with playwright and third husband Arthur Miller.

THE SURETE'S BUMBLING INSPECTOR

Swedish actress Britt Ekland was better known for her celebrity consorts than her screen performances. However, she appeared in two cult classics, *Get Carter* and *The Wicker Man*, and joined the Bond Girl club in Roger Moore's 1975 outing *The Man With The Golden Gun*. From 1963-68 she was married to Peter Sellers. By the time they met, Sellers had already used his genius for comic characters—honed on radio in *The Goon Show* —to create some memorable screen characters. He was the stroppy union representative in *I'm All Right Jack*; the premier of a British colony found to have rich mineral deposits in *Carlton-Browne of the F.O.*; the poor Indian doctor who attracts the wealthy and beautiful Sophia Loren in *The Millionairess*; and the cockney criminal mastermind in *The Wrong Arm of the Law*. 1963 saw him take on his most famous comic creation, the bumbling Inspector Clouseau in *The Pink Panther*, a role originally intended for Peter Ustinov. He returned to the Surete in four of the five sequels; Alan Arkin took over for a 1968 case, a movie which highlighted the fact that Sellers had made Clouseau his own.

OSCAR RECORD

Opposite: Meryl Streep has been nominated for an Academy Award a record thirteen times. She made an impressive screen debut in *Julia* (1977), and the following year was Oscar nominated for her performance in *The Deer Hunter*. Her first Oscar came in the tug-of-love drama *Kramer Versus Kramer* in 1979, her second award three years later for her portrayal of a woman who survived Nazi persecution in *Sophie's Choice*. Streep, a renowned perfectionist, is widely held as the most versatile and accomplished actress of the modern era, a view shared by her peers and fans alike.

Left: Gwyneth Paltrow, who married Coldplay frontman Chris Martin in 2003, gave the most tearful acceptance speech in the history of the Oscars when she picked up her award for *Shakespeare In Love* in 1999.

HERE'S TO YOU, MRS. ROBINSON

Right: Dustin Hoffmann took his time about graduating. He was 30 when he made the Mike Nichols' movie that launched his career, but his boyish looks and charm made him the perfect Benjamin, the ex-college boy inducted into the ways of the adult world by vamp-supreme Anne Bancroft. Hoffmann's next screen role, as crippled outcast Ratso in *Midnight Cowboy*, could hardly have been more different (and became the first X-certificate movie to win an Oscar). It was already clear that this new star was no Errol Flynn or John Wayne, actors who developed a screen persona and repeated the trick time and again. Hoffmann himself said he was only too pleased to hide behind the vast array of characters he portrayed—to prevent his own "boring" nature from showing.

Opposite: In 1971 Hoffmann played a meek academic pushed too far by Cornish villagers in Sam Peckinpah's *Straw Dogs*. A rape scene involving his screen wife, played by Susan George, made it one of the most controversial movies of the decade.

UNDERDOG MAKES GOOD

Left: Sylvester Stallone with Mel Gibson. Sylvester Enzio Stallone —"The Italian Stallion"—became one of Hollywood's highest paid actors playing underdog heroes. "I'm not handsome in the classical sense. The eyes droop, the mouth is crooked, the teeth aren't straight, the voice sounds like a Mafioso pallbearer, but somehow it all works" says the man who prefers to be called Sly. After making his debut in Woody Allen's *Bananas* Stallone broke into the superstar bracket with the first *Rocky* movie in 1976. He is part owner of the Planet Hollywood restaurants with friends Arnold Schwarzenegger and Bruce Willis. Willis took the part of John McClane in *Die Hard* after Stallone turned it down.

Opposite: After coming to public attention for her performance in *Body Heat*, Kathleen Turner achieved star status in her role as a romantic novelist in *Romancing the Stone*. She went on to play other leading parts in *Peggy Sue Got Married* and *The Accidental Tourist* before returning to the stage.

OSCAR AFTER 40 YEARS IN MOVIES

John Mills in uniform, solid, dependable, stiff upper-lipped, was one of the staples of the British movie industry for decades. The most famous of his war dramas, *In Which We Serve* (1942), brought together two of the most influential men in his career. Producer Noel Coward had spotted the talent of the callow Mills when he was a repertory actor and went on to cast him in numerous productions. Director David Lean was the guiding hand behind many Mills' pictures. *This Happy Breed* (1944) united all three once again, Mills playing the juvenile lead in Coward's drama of suburban life between the wars. Mills was the adult Pip in Lean's superlative 1946 adaptation of *Great Expectations*, and 25 years later their paths crossed yet again working on *Ryan's Daughter*, Mills winning a Best Supporting Oscar for his portrayal of the village idiot. He was knighted in 1977.

MARTY LANDS STEIGER WATERFRONT ROLE

Opposite: Rod Steiger's looks meant that matinée idol/romantic lead was never going to be his forte. In his 20s he was playing 50-year-old characters, though the disparity wasn't quite so great with the role that gave him his big break. Steiger was in his late 20s when he took the lead role in Paddy Chayevsky's TV play *Marty*, a story of an unattractive 34-year-old Bronx butcher looking for love. Ernest Borgnine was cast in the movie version—Steiger didn't like the strings attached to the contract—and won an Oscar; but the TV version landed Steiger the part of Marlon Brando's racketeer brother in Elia Kazan's *On The Waterfront*. He was nominated for an Oscar for his performance. Thirteen years later he won the award for his portrayal of a bigoted police chief in *In The Heat of the Night*. His favorite role was Nazerman, a New York Jew haunted by memories of prison camp life in *The Pawnbroker*.

Left: When David Niven arrived in Hollywood he was assigned a code number and a note describing him as a stock English actor (in fact, he was Scottish born). His looks, charm and wonderful voice helped to promote him, though once he became a star he was all too often given indifferent material to work with.

HOLDEN'S SUNSET BOULEVARD

Opposite: William Holden had no great fondness for acting—which is exactly why he was one of Billy Wilder's favorite stars. Wilder felt there was an understated realism in Holden's performances that raised it beyond acting. He elicited two of Holden's finest performances: as the scriptwriter who moves in with silent screen star Gloria Swanson in *Sunset Boulevard*; and as the hero of the POW drama *Stalag 17*. He received an Oscar nomination for the former and won the Best Actor award for the latter. *The Bridge On The River Kwai* (1957) made him financially secure: his fee was 10 percent of the gross, to be paid at $50,000 a year for tax reasons. As the movie made $25 million it

meant that Holden's annual cut would be rolling in for 50 years. In 1981, almost halfway into that deal, he died from blood loss following a drunken fall.

Above: Richard Gere came to prominence in the stage version of *Grease* in 1973. Ironically, John Travolta—who played Danny Zuko in the screen version—is said to have turned down the role of a male prostitute in *American Gigolo*, the movie which launched Gere's career. When he next appeared, in cool white uniform in *An Officer and a Gentleman*, Gere cemented his place among the hottest sex symbols of the 1980s.

WHO KILLED THE CHAUFFEUR?

Opposite: Bogart was not given to dalliances with his leading ladies, but during the making of *To Have And Have Not* he and 19-year-old ingenue Lauren Bacall became inseparable. The 44-year-old star's stormy third marriage, to the hard-drinking Mayo Methot, was disintegrating. When he and Bacall were reunited in the fall of 1944 to make *The Big Sleep* the chemistry was as powerful as ever, and before the year was out it was announced that his six-year marriage to Methot was over. Their second screen collaboration was a cracking thriller with a labyrinthine plot that was at times impenetrable. At one point director Howard Hawks sent a telegram to Raymond Chandler asking who'd killed the chauffeur. Chandler wired back that he had no idea.

Right: The serenely beautiful Sophia Loren.

ACKNOWLEDGMENTS

The photographs in this book are from the archives of the *Daily Mail*.
Particular thanks to Steve Torrington, Dave Sheppard,
Brian Jackson, Alan Pinnock, Katie Lee, Richard Jones and all the staff.

Thanks also to
Peter Wright, Trevor Bunting, Alison Gauntlett,
Melanie Cox, Carol Salter and Cliff Salter.
Design by John Dunne and Judy Linard.